EXPLORE MICHIGAN
LITTLE TRAVERSE BAY

George Cantor has been a journalist in the Detroit area for more than 40 years. He worked for the *Detroit Free Press* and the *Detroit News* as a baseball writer, travel writer, reporter and columnist.

His proudest achievements were covering the 1968 Detroit Tigers in their championship season, raising two beautiful daughters and seeing columns he had written years ago still hanging on refrigerator doors around the state.

He also has written 15 books on sports, travel and history.

George and his wife Sherry are residents of West Bloomfield, along with their irascible west highland terrier, Charlie.

EXPLORE MICHIGAN
LITTLE TRAVERSE BAY

An Insider's Guide to Michigan

George Cantor

The University of Michigan Press
Ann Arbor
&
Petoskey Publishing Company
Traverse City

Copyright © by George Cantor, 2005
All rights reserved
Published in the United States of America by
The University of Michigan Press
Manufactured in the United States of America
Printed on acid-free paper

2008 2007 2006 2005 4 3 2 1

ISBN 0-472-03093-0

Library of Congress Cataloging-in-publication Data on File

Explore Michigan:
Little Traverse Bay
Reviewed by The Little Traverse
Historical Society
Cover photograph provided by
Marge Beaver, Photography Plus
www.photography-plus.com

Inside photography courtesy of
Terry Phipps, 14-time Kodak
International Award Winner,
photographer of
Seasons of Little Traverse Bay
phipps@gtii.com

CONTENTS

Explore Michigan: An Insider's Guide to Michigan is not meant to be a complete listing of every restaurant or every shop; it is truly meant to be an "insider's" guide. It recommends the places that the locals, and in the case of the tourist areas, long-time summer residents, know about, frequent and recommend to their family and friends.

For example, in Traverse City, the parking meters have a button that you can hit for thirty free minutes. In Leelanau County, the National Park Service conducts winter snowshoe tours of the park. In Detroit, there are cozy restaurants that out-of-towners rarely find. And if you want a more affordable, and quiet weekend at the Grand Hotel on Mackinac Island, it is now open in early spring.

Author George Cantor has been writing travel books for over twenty years. A life-long Michigander, he has traveled and explored Michigan with the gusto it takes to make these books special. Though they are guidebooks, they make for a good read before, during and after you plan to visit. George also wanted to make sure that he really had the local flare for each book in this series, so he agreed to have locals review each book and give their comments to him.

The result is *Explore Michigan: An Insider's Guide to Michigan*, where the aerial photographs on the covers by exceptionally talented Marge Beaver invite you in. Once you start reading, you are on your way to invaluable information that puts you on the inside of what our great state has to offer.

--the publishers

LITTLE TRAVERSE BAY:
PETOSKEY-HARBOR SPRINGS
AND VICINITY

The Top Ten Don't Miss List

1. Hunt for Petoskey stones and get in some beach time at Petoskey State Park.
2. Drive the Tunnel of Trees, Highway 119, from Harbor Springs to Cross Village.
3. Ski some of the best slopes in the Midwest at Boyne Highlands or Nub's Nob.
4. Stroll and shop the Gaslight District in downtown Petoskey.
5. See the evening sun go down from Sunset Park, on U.S. 31 in Petoskey.
6. Rent a boat in Alanson or Oden and explore part of the Inland Waterway.
7. Walk out to the beacon at the entrance to Petoskey harbor for a boaters' eye view of the town.
8. Marvel at the craftsmanship of the Victorian cottages in historic Bay View.
9. Play a round on a world-class golf course at Bay Harbor or Boyne Highlands.
10. Observe the seriously large yachts at the Harbor Springs marina.

THE TURF

Sometime during the 1870s, they stopped cutting down trees long enough around here to take a good look around. From that moment on, the Little Traverse Bay area became one of the top resort destinations on the Great Lakes. After the great Chicago Fire of 1871, the local lumber industry was still shipping vast amounts of cut timber across Lake Michigan, enough to rebuild much of the devastated city. But just two years later, the Grand Rapids and Indiana Railroad, which promoted itself as "the Fishing Line," reached Petoskey. Newspapers ran wildly enthusiastic reports about the angling, healthy air and "million dollar sunsets." By 1876, the railroad was bringing members of the first resort association in the area to their new summer homes. The parade of visitors and seasonal residents has never abated.

The reason why is succinctly contained in the name of that first vacation community: Bay View. The earnest Methodists who organized it saw the place as a summer camp for personal improvement--a chance to hear lectures, listen to concerts and look to their religious life. But they also noted that remarkable vista across the bay's sparkling waters to the highlands and Seven Mile Point on the opposite shore. This alone was worth the journey. And word got out quickly.

By the 1880s, the towns of Petoskey and Harbor Springs had become favored summertime resorts of wealthy families from Chicago, Detroit, Cincinnati and all across the Midwest.

The French had been here first. They named the area L'Arbre Croche ("Crooked Tree") for a towering, gnarled fir--a landmark that could be seen from the lake, standing majestically alone high on a bluff. Jesuits established their first mission to the Ottawa, whose land this was, in 1740, in the town that is now called Cross Village.

Under American rule, much of the Little Traverse Bay area was made reservation land. It was given to the Ottawa "forever" in 1836 and closed to white settlement with only missionaries allowed in as permanent residents. But forever didn't last all that long when the ambitions of timber barons combined with political power. Harbor Springs was opened up to settlers by the 1850s. Petoskey followed over the next two decades. (The name is actually the English rendering of Petosaga, the Ottawa chief at that time.) An estimated 3,200 Native Americans still live in the area.

The resorts thrived around the first part of the 20th Century. Ever more elaborate summer homes were built. Private associations, Wequetonsing and Harbor Point among them, were formed. Several palatial hotels opened along the bayfront. But with the decline of rail travel after World War II, a sort of malaise settled over Little Traverse. Many large resorts closed. The grandchildren of longtime summer residents turned to other destinations--a bit more distant and, perhaps, a bit more glamorous and faster-paced. Starting in the 1970s, the area reinvented itself. Petoskey and Harbor Springs did makeovers of their downtown districts, capitalizing on the unique 19th Century charm that remained.

Petoskey's Gaslight District and Harbor Spring's Main Street now offer some of the best strolling and shopping in the North; an eclectic mix of fashionable apparel stores, art galleries and restaurants.

In the 1990s, an entirely new element entered the picture with the opening of Bay Harbor. An abandoned cement plant and quarry was converted into an extensive community of luxury homes and condominiums, a marina, a small downtown and one of the finest golf courses in the country.

Its success opened a new era of prosperity for the Little Traverse area, although not entirely welcomed by older residents who prefer the pace of life as it used to be.

THE TOWNS

Petoskey. This is the metropolis of Little Traverse Bay, with a population of 7,200 and the area's major concentration of motel, restaurant and retail outlets. They are clustered along the highways that bypass the town center----U.S. 31 and 131.

Petoskey rises from the south shore of the bay in a series of gentle hills. There is a sense of intimacy with the surrounding landscape and many city streets open out on stirring views across the water or nearby farmland. Mitchell Street is the main drag (accessible on a turnoff from U.S. 31), and forms the southern edge of the Gaslight District. That area's shops occupy buildings that date from the great days of the late 19th Century's lumbering boom.

Connected to the downtown area by pedestrian tunnel is Bayfront Park, a fine recreational facility that runs along the water for almost a mile.

Harbor Springs. The smaller, somewhat more exclusive (at least, in its own mind), twin sister of Petoskey. Harbor Springs works hard to keep itself wrapped in a time cocoon, retaining the look and texture of a bygone era.

The town is surrounded by upscale residential communities, many of them private, and shops line its restored Main Street. Harbor is only three blocks wide from water to hills, and its picturesque setting is a favorite for painters who set up easels at the end of the marina pier.

Bay View. This Methodist summer camp is thriving well into its second century. The playful gingerbread adornment on the Victorian homes, more than 400 in number, is an attraction in itself.

There are three inns and two restaurants open to the public on its grounds. Residents don't mind casual strollers, as long as they behave themselves, keep it quiet and leave their dogs at home.

Alanson. A pleasant resort village on the Crooked River. Its block-long downtown, on U.S. 31, is brightened by hillside flower gardens, planted along an old railroad grade. This is an excellent place at which to rent a boat and explore Crooked Lake, Crooked River and the Inland Waterway.

Pellston. Billing yourself as "America's Icebox" may not be the most effective path of self-promotion, but this is Pellston's claim to fame. Its position in a valley between two lines of hills acts as a conduit for winds blowing down from the Straits of Mackinac. On many days it challenges International Falls, Minn. for the coldest temperature in the contiguous 48 states.

The town is also the site of Pellston Regional Airport, the major commercial terminal for the northern tip of Michigan's Lower Peninsula. Northwest Airlines serves it with daily flights.

Cross Village. At the end of Michigan 119, the "Tunnel of Trees," this isolated hamlet may feel as if it's at the end of the world, as well. It has only 100 fulltime residents, many of them of Ottawa ancestry. On clear days, the outline of Beaver Island, 30 miles offshore on Lake Michigan, is visible from the bluff on which the town lies.

In summer and autumn, Cross Village fills up with travelers who explore the scenic road that leads here and linger for a bite at the famous Legs Inn.

Indian River. The town occupies an historic crossroads where the old Straits Highway—and the newer Interstate 75—cross the Inland Waterway. The Waterway was used for centuries by travelers who wanted a safe, easy way to get from Lake Huron to Lake Michigan. In the years after Indian River was settled in the 1870s, more than 30 steamboats used it on a regular commercial run.

For the last 50 years, the Waterway has been a prime pleasure boat excursion, and Indian River's position at the southeastern corner of Burt Lake has made it a nautical center.

LOCAL COLOR

Hemingway lived in this rooming house at 602 E. State Street, Petoskey.

Ernest Hemingway

The most celebrated of the area's summer residents was the world-famous author who found his voice here. Ernest Hemingway went on to win the Pulitzer and Nobel Prizes for his novels set in Spain, Africa, Italy and the waters off Cuba.

At the beginning, however, it was his short stories about Nick Adams, with their northern Michigan background, that brought him critical notice.

Most of these early works were clearly inspired by his experiences in the Petoskey area. There are those who say the time he spent in the area's drinking establishments was also a profound source of inspiration. But throughout Emmet County there are places that claim a Hemingway association, and many of their tales are even true.

He was born into a well-to-do family (his father was a doctor) in suburban Chicago in 1899, and spent 19 of the first 20 summers of his life in a cottage on nearby Walloon Lake. Windermere, is now a National Historic Site, but remains in private hands and cannot be visited. Hemingway always recalled these summers as a time of unfettered freedom. He had time to explore the countryside with friends and meet people, many of them Indians, who lay outside his regular orbit of experience. Hemingway scholars have found many of these places and individuals turning up in short stories he wrote for his high school paper.

After his stint as an ambulance driver in World War I, he returned to the scenes of his summer youth over the winter of 1919-20 in a serious effort to write fiction. He lived in a rooming house at 602 E. State Street, Petoskey, and often worked deep into the night. When old friends interrupted him too frequently, he found a refuge in Evelyn Hall, the women's dormitory at Bay View, in a room heated only by a small wood-burning stove.

Hemingway frequented the City Park Grill.

Two downtown Petoskey restaurants were Hemingway hangouts. The City Park Grill, at 432 E. Lake St., was a favorite watering hole and Jesperson's, at 312 Howard St., was acclaimed even then for its manly breakfasts.

He gave a speech on his wartime experiences that winter at the old Petoskey Public Library, on Mitchell St., and he had stayed at the Perry Hotel, on Bay St., during an earlier solo trip to the area. The Perry hosts an "Up in Michigan" week, dedicated to the works of Hemingway, every October.

His writing efforts over that Petoskey winter were largely unsuccessful, but they marked the gradual development of Adams, Hemingway's alter ego, as the narrator of his Michigan tales.

"Up in Michigan" was featured in his first book of short stories, published in 1923. Several others in that collection, including "The Doctor and the Doctor's Wife" and "Indian Camp," were based on family experiences during those boyhood summers. Several Petoskey locales also are identifiable in his first novel, "The Torrents of Spring," published in 1926.

The following year he wrote "The Sun Also Rises" and was on his way to international acclaim with a style that influenced an entire generation of authors.

Passenger Pigeons

Once there were 5 billion of them, by some estimates the most numerous species of bird on the planet. Now there are none. They were hunted into extinction in a matter of 40 years, and their last major nesting ground was near Petoskey. When that was cleaned out by hunters in 1878, the passenger pigeon was doomed.

The great naturalist John J. Audubon observed a flight of the birds in 1813. He wrote that they blocked out the sun as surely as an eclipse and continued to pass overhead "in undiminished numbers" for the next three days. He found a roost that was 40 miles long and 3 miles in width and estimated that this single flock contained more than 2 billion birds. Even as late as 1832, an Indiana ornithologist found 100 nests in a   single tree. They were thought to comprise 40 percent of the entire bird population of North America.

But the pigeons were plump and prized for their meat. They were also esteemed as game birds because of the speed of their flight, up to 70 miles an hour. Audubon wrote that each bird "Passes like a thought, and on trying to see it again, the eye searches in vain; the bird is gone." As Midwestern forests were cleared for farmland, much of the best nesting grounds for the bird disappeared. When the last great concentration of nests was found in the Petoskey area, it set off a frenzy of killing. Around 5,000 hunters and netters made their way here, and when they were done millions of the birds were dead. About 300 tons were shipped to market.

Even at the time, it was understood that with the slaughter in Petoskey the species had been virtually destroyed. Smaller nesting grounds were found in Wisconsin and Ohio, but by 1900 they, too, had been wiped out. The last known passenger pigeon died in captivity in the Cincinnati Zoo in 1914.

Petoskey Stones

It is something of a misnomer. The name for these fossilized corals was attached to Petoskey because this is where 19th Century souvenir hunters first began to find, collect and polish them.

Actually, Petoskey stones can be found across the upper Midwest, as far away as Iowa, and even have turned up in northern Europe, but Petoskey claimed naming rights and Michigan recognized the connection by designating them as the state stone in 1965. It was the first state to give a fossil official status.

The stones are approximately 350 million years old, give or take a few. This was the Devonian Age when our planet looked a good deal different than it does now. When the stones were formed, Michigan lay beneath a warm prehistoric sea, situated south of the Equator. Over the millennia, vast tectonic shifts moved continents to new places on the globe. Michigan drifted north and upwards, so that its present surface is part of what was once an underwater coral reef.

Coral is a living creature and these fossils once had soft tissue at their core. But the living cells were replaced by silt and mud which turned into calcite and silica. The result is a stone that is distinctly marked with the outline of the coral colony. The fossilized stones became embedded in glaciers. When they receded, at the end of the last Ice Age, the Petoskeys were left on lakeshores and gravel deposits. The polishing action of the lake waves makes them easier to find on area beaches. The best time to look is after a rain or immediately following the ice break-up in spring.

Petoskey State Park is the best known hunting grounds for rockhounds. Another promising spot is **Magnus City Park,** at the end of W. Lake Street, across U.S. 31 from downtown Petoskey.

The locals prefer a more isolated place, right behind the Glen's Market mall, north of the city on U.S. 31. Either drive through the mall to its rear entrance or turn towards the bay on Hampton Street from the highway. There is a parking area, a bike trail and a small lookout point with outstanding views towards the dunes of the state park. A rather steep path leads down to the water and a small rocky beach where the stones can be found quite easily.

For those who want a souvenir without the effort, there are several shops in Petoskey that offer polished stones. Best known of these is Grandpa Shorter's in the Gaslight District. A bit more out of the way is Lake Michigan Rock-Gem, a place that sets the stones in arrangements for clocks and pen sets. It is located at 5179 Pickerel Lake Road, off U.S. 31 on the way to Conway.

Robert Emmet

He never set foot in the place, but the county which surrounds Little Traverse Bay is named for this Irish patriot. The State Legislature came up with the name in 1842, when the area was first divided into governing units.

The well-born Emmet, still in his 20s, led a doomed attempt to seize Dublin Castle and spark a revolt against British rule. He was executed in 1803, but his dramatic speech at the gallows fired Irish imaginations and became a staple of patriotic recitations. "Let no man write my epitaph," he declared, "until Ireland had won its freedom."

This county was originally called Tonedagana, a name dreamed up by Indian agent Henry Schoolcraft, who loved concocting words that sounded vaguely Native American. The legislature, mindful, perhaps, of the growing presence of Irish voters in the state, decided to honor Emmet instead.

WHERE TO STAY

The Inn at Bay Harbor

Top of the Line

The Inn at Bay Harbor. In the Bay Harbor complex, on U.S. 31. (231) 439-4000.

Built in the style of a classic 19th Century resort, the Inn offers its guests the view that full-time Bay Harbor residents pay hundreds of thousands of dollars to get. Room prices accordingly are the highest in the area. Expect to pay more than $300 a night in summer season for rooms with a view, and substantially more than that for larger suites.

Those who choose to ante up will receive top-grade service with all the amenities (except for the unfortunate, but temporary, omission of an indoor swimming pool). There is an outdoor pool, beach, fully equipped spa and access to some of the best golf courses in the state. Since 2004, the 134-room hotel has been part of the Renaissance group of Marriott Hotels.

Boyne Highlands Resort. Harbor Springs.
North from Michigan 119 by way of Pleasantview Road. (231) 549-6000.

A family-friendly place, surrounded by forest and hills. The Highlands was built as a ski lodge but morphed over the years into a golf resort, too. Rooms in the alpine-style main building are a bit dark. A better bet for families is the condos in the Heather Hills section of the complex; they are spacious and feature an indoor pool, an important amenity for travelers with children in this changeable northern climate. There is also a good outdoor pool at the lodge, with an adjacent clock tower that plays little tunes on the quarter hour.

There are 54 holes of golf on the property, 50 ski slopes and 414 rooms. Summer prices start in the $125 range for rooms in the lodge.

A Touch of History

Stafford's Bay View Inn. U.S. 31. (800) 258-1886.

The 31-room hotel on the Bay View property dates from 1886. While the Bay View community opens only during the summer, the inn operates all year, and is especially nice in winter when it offers sleigh rides through the snow-covered, Christmas card streets.

The three-story building with central cupola features a restaurant that serves all meals but is best known for an outstanding Sunday brunch, June through October. The inn is less than one block from the bay. A distraction, however, is its location on a portion of U.S. 31 that can be quite congested on summer weekends. But its charms amply compensate for that.

The Stafford's Bay View Inn in Harbor Springs

Rooms start at just over $100 and are priced in the mid $200s for the nine fireplace suites, though cheaper off-season. Full breakfast included.

Terrace Inn. Bay View. 1549 Glendale, in the middle of the Bay View community. (800) 530-9898.

The inn features one of the most dramatic entryways in the area; a long flight of stairs leading up to an expansive front veranda. For those who choose to forego the climb, a side entry accommodates cars. There is, however, no interior elevator.

The Terrace was opened in 1911 and emphasizes the "Somewhere in Time" sense of the past. One of its suites is, in fact, named for that movie which was filmed in northern Michigan. Its rooms do not have telephones or televisions, but the porch is generously supplied with rockers. Situated two blocks off U.S. 31, it is perfect for those who treasure quiet, but also would like access to Bay View's private beach. There are 43 rooms, a restaurant noted for its planked whitefish dinners and prices are a bit lower than those at the Bay View Inn. Open all year.

The Stafford's Perry Hotel in Petoskey

Stafford's Perry Hotel. Bay at Lewis Streets, Petoskey. (800) 737-1899.

This is the last of the grand resort hotels in this area. Built in 1899, it wears its years with renewed grace after extensive remodeling over the last decade.

It is named for its original owner, Dr. Norman Perry, a local dentist who decided he'd rather tickle palates than drill molars. It was expanded to its present size in the 1920s by a second owner, the Reycraft family, which ran it for 42 years. Since the early 90s it has been operated by the Stafford Hospitality Group.

Its formal restaurant is noted for Great Lakes fish dinners and its casual basement dining area, The Noggin Room, is another of the many authentic Ernest Hemingway hangouts in town. The Perry is just a few blocks from the Gaslight District in downtown Petoskey and many of its 80 rooms have bay views.

Bed and Breakfasts

Gingerbread House. Bay View. On U.S. 31. (231) 347-3538. This four-room cottage gives visitors the chance to stay in an actual Bay View residence. The

Gingerbread House, named for the prevailing architectural style in the community, was converted to a B&B in 1988, which was 107 years after it was built. All rooms overlook the bay, but go for the Victoria, with its French doors opening onto a private balcony. That is where you can truly recapture a sense of what life was like for the occupants in another century.

The house is open from mid-May through October, and there is a two-night minimum on weekends.

Inn at Crooked Lake. Oden. On U.S. 31. (877) 644-3339.

The lovely inland lake is right across the road from this restored 1906 summer cottage. Oden is a tiny lakeside community, less than a 10-minute drive from the middle of Petoskey or Harbor Springs.

The 5-room inn is noted for farm-fresh breakfasts, evening wine tastings and carbohydrates-be-damned dessert trays served around the fireplace.

Innkeepers Diane and Mark Hansell say their most popular room is the Mackinac, with its pine sleigh bed and antique claw-foot tub.

Serenity. 504 Rush St., Petoskey. (877) 347-6171.

The ideal choice for those looking for what the name of this B&B promises. Serenity is situated on a hilltop, a few blocks from the Gaslight District and downtown Petoskey, with views of the bay from its three rooms. The best is (naturally) the Bayview Room.

The house dates from 1890 and among its most attractive features are the two large glassed-in porches. Innkeepers Ed and Marjorie Mehney have also planted some exceptionally pleasant gardens on the property.

Rohm House and Farm. 10950 Rogers Road, Burt Lake (888) 895-7411.

This is a more contemporary house, but its location on a tranquil hillside overlooking Burt Lake gives it a strong

sense of times gone by. Rohn House is surrounded by a
63-acre farm, and its three rooms have views of either the
water or orchards.

Proprietor Robin Rohm, who worked in the fashion
industry in New York for 29 years, hopes eventually to
open a design studio in the house. The B&B is open all
year, with hiking and snowshoeing available in the adjacent
fields. It is located about midway between Alanson and
Indian River; off M-68 at southbound McMichael Road,
then an immediate right on Rogers Road.

An Offbeat Choice

Harborside Inn. 266 E. Main St., Harbor Springs.
(231) 526-6238.

A condo hotel. It is located right in downtown Harbor
Springs, in the middle of the shopping area, close to the
beach and restaurants. Views of the bay open out from its
rooftop and every room has its own terrace. Breakfast only.

For Families

Apple Tree Inn. (231) 348-2900. **Baywinds Inn.**
(231) 347-4193.

These two diamond motor inns are located right next to
each other along U.S. 131, south of Petoskey. They are convenient to moderately priced eating places, malls and
movies. Both also feature indoor pools. They are quite popular so reserve early, especially on weekends.

Condos

Several condominium communities at Bay Harbor and
other private resorts offer weekly rentals, a good alternative
for families on longer stays. Almost all of them are
equipped with kitchens.

The Cottages at Crooked Tree, situated on a golf course
on the heights across the highway from Bay Harbor, and

Lakeside Cottages, located adjacent to the Inn at Bay Harbor, can be reserved by calling (231) 439-4000. Both have two and three bedroom units.

Condos at the Cliffs section of Bay Harbor are a bit larger, have a more convenient location and that famous view across the bay. They are rented through the Lloyd D. Pedersen brokerage at (877) 492-1022.

An assortment of other condos in the area are handled by a central agency, **Sylvain Management Co.** (800) 678-1036.

Among their best placed properties are:

Trout Creek is located near the ski and golf resorts of Nub's Nob and Boyne Highlands, off Pleasantview Road. There are in-room spas, indoor and outdoor pools, tennis and programs for the kids in summer. (800) 748-0245.

Harbor Cove is a collection of townhouses spread over a wooded area, just off Beach Road, near Harbor Springs. There is a private beach on the bay, tennis, pools and nature trails.

Camping

Petoskey State Park, immediately off M-119, has two campground facilities; Tannery Creek with 98 sites and the Dunes, which is a bit more rustic, with 70. There are, in addition, two small cabins the park also offers for rent.

The campgrounds are open from April through November, with electricity and toilet facilities unavailable the first and last months. This is a very popular facility and it fills up fast in the summer. Reservations should be made several months in advance at (800) 447-2757.

Burt Lake State Park is also a highly coveted location, requiring advance plans for reservations at the above phone

number. It is on the lake of the same name, just west of
Indian River, and its 374 campsites feature modern facilities
from May to mid-October. There is also one cabin that
sleeps four. There is a short hiking trial and access to the
lake, which has a beach and is regarded as one of the top
fishing venues in the area.

Magnus Park is run by the city of Petoskey, with 72
sites on Little Traverse Bay. It accommodates both tents and
full hook-ups for RVs. There is a 1,000-foot long beach,
picnic areas and it is known for its bountiful Petoskey
stones. In addition, it is just a short walk along W. Lake
Street to the middle of downtown and Bayfront Park. Open
May through late October. Call (231) 347-1027.

Camp Petosega is a bit more secluded, on Pickerel Lake,
south of Alanson. There are 32 campsites, with new show-
ers and restrooms, a recreation hall and electric hookups.
Five cabins, priced according to size at $20 to $70, are
available. There is also a small beach.

From Alanson, head east on M-68 and then south on
Banwell Road for 6 miles. (231) 347-6536.

More rustic camping experiences are available in the
Mackinaw State Forest's three campgrounds. Haakwood
and Weber Lake both have 18 campsites, while Maple Bay
has 38. Only the basic campsite is offered and there are no
reservations, but all are located on water.

Haakwood is beside the Sturgeon River, south of Indian
River, along the Straits Highway (also called Old U.S. 27).

Weber Lake is situated on that small lake, just off C-58,
west of Wolverine, on Weber Lake Road. It is also the base
for an extensive series of hiking and biking trails.

Maple Bay is located near the Maple River's outlet into
Burt Lake. There is a beach, a boat ramp and outstanding
opportunities for both river and lake fishing. It is located
off Brutus Road, east of the town of Brutus.

EATING OUT

Fish from neighboring waters is the star attraction here, especially whitefish and walleye. Planked whitefish, in which the filet is served on a wooden board and surrounded by mashed potatoes and veggies, is a northern Michigan standby. Most of these places have more ambitious dishes, too, but you can't go wrong with these choices.

Little Traverse Bay Restaurant. Harbor Springs. (231) 526-7800. Situated high on a hill, behind the first tee of the adjoining golf course, with breath-taking views across the bay from its windows and outdoor terrace. This is a favorite of longtime summer residents, many of whom choose to celebrate weddings and anniversaries on its scenic grounds. It is also a solid value, with most entrees priced in the $20 range and includes a salad course, an increasing rarity in this area.

It's a bit tricky to find. From Highway 119, turn right on Conway Road and then an immediate left on Clayton. Follow this road past the first stop sign, curve to the right a short way and then head left, up the hill to the restaurant.

The Fish. Harbor Springs. (231) 526-3969.

It's a bit out of the way, adjacent to Mackinaw State Forest, north of town. Take State Street (C77) and follow it to the junction with Stutsmanville Road.

Those who make the drive will be rewarded with simply and carefully prepared seafood dishes, both from local waters and of the ocean variety. It is a clean, uncluttered place with views of the woods next door from its windows.

Stafford's Pier. Harbor Springs. (231) 526-6201.

As you might have guessed, the Pier is right on the water and has a nautical décor. From the main dining room, the Pointer Room, there are views of the Harbor Springs marina to complement a wide-ranging menu, which is reliably consistent on its fish and chicken dishes.

The more informal Chart Room has many of the same entrees but no view and lower prices. An outdoor deck in summer features lighter fare. It is located at State and Bay streets, in downtown Harbor Springs.

Douglas Lake Steak House. Pellston. (231) 539-8588.
True to its name, red meat is the star of this menu, especially a terrific steak au poivre. But there is a good sampling of fish dishes, too, in a cozy log cabin overlooking a quiet lake. Take Douglas Lake Road, which heads due east from the Pellston Airport, and keep driving until you reach the water. Closed November and April.

Latitude. Bay Harbor. (231) 439-2750.
At the edge of the Bay Harbor shopping district, with picture windows in its second floor dining room overlooking the marina.

High priced and innovative, it is where the people take guests they want to impress. This is one of the top places in the area. Entrees are always imaginatively presented and feature locally-grown foods. Service is excellent.

Chandler's. Petoskey. (231) 347-2981.
In a secluded courtyard on Howard St., in the midst of the Gaslight District, is this tiny place with a growing list of devotees who would prefer to keep it a secret. Too late for that.

At lunch it is a moderately priced establishment, with a limited menu of sandwiches and salads and some outdoor seating. But at dinner it is transformed into a highly ambitious restaurant, serving what is best described as global cuisine; adapting locally grown products to surprisingly eclectic international choices. Located just a few steps north of Lake St.

Legs Inn. Cross Village. (231) 526-2281.
This place is a destination in itself, lying at the end of the scenic Tunnel of Trees on Highway 119, along the Lake Michigan shore. It was the creation of Stanley Smolak, a Polish

The popular Legs Inn in Cross Village.

immigrant who moved to northern Michigan in the 1920s, became intrigued with Native American culture and decided to build a place that was in harmony with his understanding of that way of life.

Smolak's timber and stone structure was put together from driftwood, tree stumps, rocks and any other material he could find in the neighborhood. The result is a building that is both whimsical and inspiring. It got its name from the stove legs that decorate the parapet around the building.

In keeping with Smolak's ancestry, the menu has a definitive Polish accent. It features Old World dishes such as potato pancakes, pierogi and blinis. You don't walk away from here hungry.

Prices are moderate and in good weather there is outdoor dining in gardens that overlook the lake. Legs Inn is open from mid-May to mid-October. Polish staffers work all summer long here.

Teddy Griffin's Roadhouse. Harbor Springs.
(231) 526-7805. If they played hockey in Ireland the result would probably be a Dublin restaurant that looked very

much like this. Its motto, "Better food than most hospitals," says it all--a place that doesn't take itself too seriously and offers lots of fun for the money. It also has a sign that says, "If you like home cooking, eat at home."

Opened by a sports-happy Detroit restaurant owner, Teddy Griffin's is convenient to the ski resorts of Boyne Highlands and Nub's Nob, and only 10 minutes from the middle of Harbor Springs and Petoskey. Walleye, perch and ribs are the big deals here while diners can take in Detroit Red Wings memorabilia and Irish lore. Many professional hockey players can be seen here.

Follow Pleasantview Road north from Highway 119 to the turnoff to Boyne Highlands.

Lighter Bites

Jesperson's. 312 Howard Street. Petoskey.

Serving up breakfasts for over a century. The only drawback to having that meal here is that you don't get to sample one of their trademark pies. So there's always lunch. Situated in the Gaslight District, on Howard St., between Lake and Mitchell. Very famous for the pies—especially cherry berry. Many people will have their pies shipped to them across the country. Early bird gets the worm.

Roast & Toast. 309 Lake Street. Petoskey.

The top coffee house in town, jammed with locals during lunch for outstanding soups and sandwiches. A good assortment of baked goods, too, at breakfast. It's also in the Gaslight District, on Lake Street, a few yards east of Petoskey St. There is an outdoor deck in the back with a glimpse of the bay.

Bob's Place. 7515 U.S. 31. Alanson.

Just what a small town gathering place should be. Smack on the main street (U.S. 31), serving up great burgers, a little Mexican food and, by its own estimate, 100 varieties of soup. But, hey, who's counting? Try the prime rib—they're famous for it.

Turkey's. 250 Main Street. Harbor Springs.
No, it isn't the place to go at Thanksgiving. The place was opened by a local athlete and that was his nickname. Good choice for kids, with pizza and sandwiches at dinner. In the shopping area, on Main St.

Juilleret's. 130 State Street. Harbor Springs.
Offered for historic interest. It's been doing business at the same downtown stand since 1895 when it opened as an ice cream parlor. During the 1920s, it was also a dancehall, and the song "Sleepytime Gal" was written by Ange Lorenzo when he led the band here one summer. A hangout for the local summer residents, it does come under the heading of "landmark." It's on State St., just up from Bay. The planked white fish is spectacular, though don't forget to try to be a member of the Big J Club. For dessert try the thundercloud or the velvet, and don't count the calories.

Dutch Oven, 7611 US-31. Alanson.
It's been around for 70 years so they must be doing something right at this small town institution. Great European-style baked goodies, and a yarn shop under the same roof. It's right on U.S. 31.

Bob-In Again. 1150 Bay View Road. Petoskey.
A 50-style diner with a pretty basic menu. But the home-made frozen custard is outstanding and that's what brings in the crowds. You can eat inside, at a table or counter, or at picnic benches in the open air. It's on U.S. 31, just south of Bay View. A short walk to a great sunset.

Gurney's. 215 E. Main Street. Harbor Springs.
It's carry-out only at this little deli on Main Street. But around lunch time the line is out the door to grab one of

the made-to-order sandwiches for a picnic. Great selection of cold cuts and cheeses.

Mary Ellen's. 145 E. Main Street. Harbor Springs.
This is another Main Street fixture in this resort town, with a genuine old time soda fountain serving up ice cream treats along with sandwiches at lunch. Don't miss the chocolate malts. Also serves breakfast.

Vivio's. 3301 Chippewa Beach Road. Indian River.
Casual Italian in a long cabin with a full compliment of deer heads on the wall. A good choice for pizza, but it offers more complex menu items, too. It's on the Straits Highway (Old 27), just south of Michigan 68.

CITY WALKS

Petoskey: From the Gaslights to the Bay

A corner street in Petoskey.

This walk will give you a sampling of the city's natural beauty and its consumer-oriented attractions, too. Parking can be tight in downtown Petoskey during the summer season. The best strategy is to leave your car in the large city lot (now with a sign calling it **Elk's Lot**) on Lake St., a block and a half east of Howard. It is metered, though, so watch your time.

When you walk out of the lot onto Lake, the **City Park Grill** (ask for the Hemingway handout) will be across the street to your left. This is one of the most famous and authentic of the Ernest Hemingway hangouts in town. In his time it was called the **Park Garden.** He enjoyed watching illegal bare-knuckle prize fights in its outdoor gardens. The place has toned down a lot since then, although you wonder at the primal instincts aroused by some of the rock bands that play here on weekends.

The antique hand-carved bar and pressed tin ceiling are worth a look inside and the kitchen serves up the finest biscuits in town, too.

To the right is **Pennsylvania Park.** The tracks have long been out of use, but the park still bears the name of the **Penn Central Railroad** that once ran there. Built in 1875 but destroyed by fire 24 years later. Summer concerts (excellent for picnic breaks) are held at the bandstand near the center of the two-block long park, usually on Tuesday and Friday afternoons and Tuesday evening. It is also the site of art and antiques festivals.

Follow the park to Mitchell Street and turn right across the tracks. Notice the **Flatiron Deli,** near the corner of Howard. The building had to assume the odd three-cornered shape in order to stay out of the way of the passing trains.

Cross Mitchell and walk two blocks down to State. At the corner is **St. Francis Xavier Church.** With its soaring central spire, this is the town's most visible landmark and one of the most beautiful houses of worship in northern Michigan. The history of this parish goes back to 1859, with the establishment of St. Francis Solanus Mission. The oldest building in Petoskey, it still stands near the bayfront on W. Lake Street.

As the parish grew, its church moved to a Howard Street location, and the present structure was completed after a five-year construction period in 1908. Labor and material were donated by local residents, many of them the ancestors of present day parishioners. Step inside to see the vaulted ceilings, frescoes and stained glass windows. You will understand why the church is so much in demand for weddings by Catholics from across the state.

A renovation in 2001 was bitterly and vocally opposed by those who feared its historic qualities would be diminished. But the year-long restoration seemed to leave all parties mollified, if not entirely happy.

Turn left on State to enter one of the historic residential areas of the city, filled with rambling old homes that were built during the lumbering boom of the late 19th Century. At the southeast corner of State and Woodland is the house in which **Hemingway** rented a room during the winter of 1919-20 as he endeavored to become a serious writer of fiction.

Continue on State to Lockwood, turn left and then left again on Michigan to complete this turn through the historic district. Then turn right at Woodland, and at Mitchell take a short jog to the left and cross the street onto Division.

On the left is the **Crooked Tree Art Center,** housed in the former United Methodist Church. The Gothic Revival building, dating from 1890, has been lovingly restored by the Center. The sanctuary, with original stained glass, is now a 260-seat theater, where performances are put on throughout the year. There is also an exhibit area for visiting art shows and several workshops and studios.

Follow Division two more blocks to Bay and turn left. Just across the railroad tracks is the **Perry Hotel,** the sole surviving 19th Century resort in the area. It was the first brick hotel in Petoskey and it's worth a turn around in the lobby to admire the fine restoration.

A short walk along Bay and then a left on Howard will bring you into the middle of the **Gaslight District,** one of the finest shopping areas in the state. There are some national retailers here, but most of the stores are personalized places, with goods meant for an upscale buyer. Notice that many of them have outlets in the warm weather resorts of Florida and Arizona, too. Little Traverse Bay attracts the same crowd in summer.

At the corner of Howard and Lake, go inside **Symons General Store.** The oldest commercial structure in town (it opened in 1879), it still has the air of a cracker-barrel-around-the-stove country sort of place. That's a bit deceptive because its downstairs wine selection and assortment of cheeses is the most far-ranging in the area.

Turn left on Lake to pass more of the district's shops. At the end of this block is **Grandpa Shorter's,** which has been in operation as a souvenir store since 1880. Its first proprietor was Petosega, the very same Ottawa leader for whom the city is named. It is also a choice outlet for Petoskey stones.

Turn right on Petoskey and at the end of the block look for the pedestrian tunnel that leads underneath busy U.S. 31 to **Bayfront Park.** The 65-foot tall clock tower, the park's central feature, will be right in front of you.

Straight ahead is the marina and fishing pier. A walk to the right will take you past the softball diamond, the scene of championship tournaments during summer, and then on a pedestrians-only jaunt along a path running between the bluffs and the water. You can even see a waterfall come tumbling over the cliff.

If you choose to head left, the **Little Traverse History Museum** (see the Museums section) will be directly in your path. A large, green meadow leads to a footbridge across the Bear River, which empties into the bay here. The walkway out to the harbor beacon begins past the bridge.

The walk ends there, with a view of Petoskey perched atop its bluff on one side and sails on the sunlit bay on the other.

Harbor Springs: Down Main Street

The frozen harbor in Harbor Springs.

It is hard to get lost in Harbor Springs. Bay on one side, hills on the other, with three streets running parallel to each other in between--simplicity itself.

The tough part is finding a parking place. Because of this straight and narrow geography, space is severely limited and it may be nearly impossible to find an open spot in the downtown area. If that's the case, the best thing to do is retrace your route on Main Street (Highway 119, on which you probably entered town) and grab the first space you find.

Besides, the residential portion of Main St., with its expansive white frame homes, is a pleasant walk in itself. On the 300 East Main block, look for the **hexagonal Shay House,** built in 1888 by the inventor of a logging locomotive. Right next door is the **Chief Andrew Blackbird Home** (see Museums).

Harbor Springs works hard to keep its image bright. Some of America's wealthiest families have been summering here for generations and they do not welcome jarring change. The town did win several national awards in the 1970s for brightening up its formerly dowdy downtown, but that was a change that enriched its Victorian setting.

Its three-block long shopping area, along Main and Bay streets, is heavy on antiques and art galleries. Take Main to State, turn left and then a left on Bay to get the flavor of it. Many artists choose to work here because of the physical setting and the strong Native American heritage. At one time it had the highest concentration of Indian residents in the state.

Turn left from Bay at Gardner and retrace your steps with a left onto Main. At the far end of the street is the steeple of **Holy Childhood of Jesus Church,** an institution that goes back to the very roots of the community. It was established in 1829 as St. Peter's, a mission church and school for the Ottawa, and was given its present name in 1851 after an expansion. For more than a century, until the 1980s, it operated as a Native American boarding school. Holy Childhood now runs a day care center for the entire community, but during a remodeling in the late 1990s efforts to enhance its legacy through the use of Ottawa symbolism and designs were added to the interior. Walk inside for a look.

Between the church and the water is **Zorn Park,** a favorite picnic ground and the site of arts and crafts shows during the summer. A small sandy beach lies at the bayside.

Head back to town along Bay Street. Just past **Stafford's Pier restaurant** is the walkway out to the marina. This is the deepest harbor on the Great Lakes and it can accommodate some very impressive craft. Walk out to the end of the pier for an artist's view of the little town, and a good idea of why it has remained a treasure among those who seek vistas of the past.

Bay View

There are organized walking tours of Bay View each Wednesday and Thursday, from early July to mid-August, led by a fourth generation resident of the community. They run a bit more than an hour and a quarter and are well worth taking.

The Wednesday tours leave from the lobby of the Terrace Inn at 1 p.m. On Thursdays they depart from **Stafford's Bay View Inn,** at the same time. Reservations can be made at (231) 526-8888.

There are fascinating tales about Hemingway, who used the grounds as a winter retreat, and how the temperance crusades of Carrie Nation influenced the early residents.

If that's a bit too formal for your taste, or if you're not going to be in the area in the middle of the week, you can still enjoy this gingerbread wonderland on your own.

Leave northbound U.S. 31 at Encampment. This street forms an oval at the heart of Bay View. Leave your car near the base of the stairway to the **Terrace Inn** and go explore.

Bay View began in 1876 as an actual campground. Its attendees, members of Michigan's Methodist Church, lived in tents. Its original purpose was religious study, but within a decade it had evolved into a Midwestern Chautauqua. Artists and political figures, such as Booker T. Washington, were invited to deliver lectures, and the concert series, which continues to this day, was initiated.

The grounds were platted and homes built, descending on gently curving streets from the heights of 200 feet down to the bay.

There are two concert and theater venues on the grounds, **Voorhies Hall** and **Hall Auditorium,** both of them a few steps from the oval. Summer programs run from late June to mid-August. A schedule and tickets are available through the Bay View Music Festival at (231) 348-9551.

But the big treat for the casual visitor is just taking in the lost-in-time setting and the marvelous craftsmanship of the old houses. Many of them look as if the woodcarvers were paid by the curlicue. The entire community, which is open from May through October, was declared a **National Historic Landmark** in 1987.

DRIVING TOURS

U.S. 31----Charlevoix County Line to Oden

This is a part of the **Mackinaw Highway,** one of the first designated national routes in the old federal road system. It runs, eventually, from the Mackinac Bridge to Mobile, Ala. In Michigan, its course is down the eastern

Lake Michigan shore.

In some portions of the state U.S. 31 is well out of sight of the big lake. But through this area, the water is almost always visible.

The five-mile long **Bay Harbor** development will be on the left immediately after entering Emmet County. Once past its **Marina Shopping Area** and the **Cliffs,** watch for the turnout to **East Park.** This vantage point will give you a great view over the entire sweep of **Little Traverse Bay** and across to **Harbor Springs.**

The route makes a sharp left turn at the junction with U.S. 131. Once across the **Bear River bridge,** Petoskey's Bayfront Park will be on the left. The road runs on a bluff above the water here, another especially scenic portion.

Watch for the turnoff to the left for **Sunset Park.** The parking area begins filling up with spectators in the early evening. The show is spectacular, as the sun sinks into the lake and fills the horizon with purple and orange ribbons. Some families make it an occasion for a late picnic, too. (Summer sunsets come late here because you are at the very western edge of the Eastern Time Zone. It will be well after 9:15 in late June through midJuly.) The highway then heads through the middle of Bay View and its gingerbread cottages.

After a brief run through a congested commercial strip, U.S. 31 turns away from the lake. In a few miles, it reaches Conway and the shore of Crooked Lake, with a scenic run along this inland body of water and into the town of Oden.

Beach Road and Highway 119---Petoskey to Cross Village

Michigan 119 branches off from U.S. 31 just north of Bay View. It passes Petoskey State Park, and just beyond Tapperooney's Restaurant watch for the turnoff to Beach Street, the only thoroughfare going to the left. This narrow road passes through a small forest preserve and emerges on the north shore of Little Traverse Bay, which it then follows into Harbor Springs on a satisfying scenic course.

Before you reach the town, however, turn left at

Ramona Park. This was the name of a resort hotel that once stood here. The place was notorious for its casino, which attracted many Chicago baddies in the 1920s and stood vacant as a crumbling landmark for many years. The site is now occupied by private residences.

This road now heads into the **Wequetonsing Association.** This is another of the private communities that were created in the late 19th Century for the monetarily favored. The grounds are private but you can pass through on this road to get a glimpse of the spectacular summer cottages that face the water.

One of many beautiful drives in Little Traverse Bay.

As you enter Harbor Springs, the road ends at the tiny parking area for the **Zoll Street Beach.** Take a right on Zoll, then an immediate left on Bay to reach downtown along the waterfront. Continue on Bay to State Street, then turn right. After one block, this street rejoins Highway 119 and begins its journey to **Cross Village.**

Give yourself plenty of time for this drive. The road twists and turns as it follows the cliffs above **Lake Michigan** and you'll want to pull over at one of the viewing areas to get a more leisurely look. These areas are infrequent and not well marked, so be alert for them when they come.

Summer homes cling to the side of the bluff or rest atop adjacent hills. The old hardwood forest forms a dense canopy high overhead. Glimpses of the lake open out every few yards. Many travel writers regard this as the most scenic drive in Michigan, but it is only for the patient.

The recommended meal stop in Cross Village is **Legs Inn.** But if that doesn't suit you, or if the time in not convenient, look for the sign to Highway 77 and head south on that road for a fast return trip.

It runs through rolling farmland and a part of the **Mackinaw State Forest,** eventually ending up in the middle of Harbor Springs. Or you can take a left turn from this highway on Stutsmanville Road, then a right on Pleasantview Road for a more scenic alternative route. This drive is absolutely magnificent in early October.

Great Views Along the Way

1. Sunset Park, Petoskey.
2. Observation deck on the bike trail behind Glen's Market, U.S. 31, north of Petoskey.
3. From the terrace of Little Traverse Bay restaurant, Harbor Springs.
4. Swing Bridge on the Crooked River, Alanson.
5. Bill's Farm Market, east from Petoskey on C-58.
6. Thorne Swift Nature Preserve, off M-119, on Lower Shore Drive, north of Harbor Springs.
7. Old Baldy Dunes trail, Petoskey State Park.
8. East Park, Petoskey.
9. Bayfront Park Marina, Petoskey.
10. Harbor Springs Marina.

SHOPPING

Petoskey's Gaslight District and Harbor Springs' Main Street are the foremost shopping areas, and they are described in the chapter on walks through those towns.

Marina District, Bay Harbor, off U.S. 31.

The intent of Bay Harbor's developers was to recreate the look of a late 19th Century resort. The residential and commercial architecture follows that pattern, complete to the block-long downtown shopping area. It does make for a very nice day of shopping, though don't come here looking for bargains. This is a high rent district and prices are pegged to match. These stores are big on resort wear, jewelry and art galleries.

Hungry families come to breakfast at the **Original Pancake House,** part of a national chain. There is also ice cream at the **Sunflower Café** and carry-out treats at the **Galley Gourmet.** This is also the locale of the more formal **Latitudes.**

Latitudes restaurant located at Bay Harbor.

At the end of the block is the Bay Harbor marina with a regular assortment of nice boats.

For a pleasant short walk, head past the Bay Harbor real estate offices, at the opposite end of the block from the marina, and stroll along the bayshore, past an artificial lagoon, to the Inn at Bay Harbor.

Toski Sands, on Highway 119, between Petoskey and Harbor Springs.

A very useful little strip mall. There's a grocery with an excellent selection of fresh meat and gourmet items. Johan's

Bakery, a coffee shop, a fast food place, Scalawags, specializing in whitefish lunches.

This is a pleasant stop for a snack and a place to stock up for a barbecue or picnic. You can also put in an order for a naturally grown turkey, which many locals do for Thanksgiving or a special meal.

Bill's Farm Market, on Mitchell Road (C 58), east of Petoskey.

This is the best place in the area for fresh produce, and a treat merely to walk through. Bill McMaster grows most of the fruits and vegetables he sells here on his family's 150-acre farm. Nothing too exotic, just an astonishing variety of local staples, such as corn and melons and cherries and squash.

The location itself is worth the drive. The market is set in the midst of rolling hill country, a serene landscape that will remind some observers of the Cotswolds in England. Be sure to walk inside for the selection of home-made jams, too.

The market opens from June into December, when it offers trees and wreaths for the holidays.

Bluff Gardens, 721 W. Lake Road, Harbor Springs. (231) 526-5571.

Over 70 years old, they are known to all the local restaurants and local cooks as the place to find miniature vegetables—you have to see them to believe it. Bring your checkbook, because they aren't cheap, but it is worth it. They also have house made preserves and salsas, and hand-painted Faience pottery.

Offbeat and Off the Center

Mary Ann Archer Jewelry, on Highway 119 in the Harbor Plaza, adjacent to the Harbor Springs Airport.

A Saginaw native, Archer lived for many years in Santa Fe, and the southwestern influence is evident in her designs.

Since her return to Michigan, she has developed a devoted following in this area.

Sturgeon River Pottery, U.S. 31, opposite Bay Harbor.
At first glance, this looks like a fanciful overgrown chicken coop. But a look inside will reveal a remarkable collection of stoneware, hand-crafted on the premises. There is also a fine assortment of folk crafts, including bird houses and furniture, from the area. The place for birders—period.

Three Pines Studio, C 66 at State Road, Cross Village.
This place specializes in the work of Emmet County artists. More than 40 of them exhibit here. Many times you will see artists working on their art when you are there.

McLean and Eakin Booksellers, 307 E. Lake Street, Petoskey.
A nicely old fashioned, personalized sort of bookstore, where the employees know their stuff and works of local interest are featured. New York publishers' reps are always keeping an eye on what's selling here to see what's hot. Winner of the Charles S. Haslam Award for Excellence in Bookselling.

Between the Covers, 152 Main Street, Harbor Springs.
A community bookshop with an outstanding selection of contemporary fiction, mystery, children's and regional titles, staffed by friendly readers, where they are always ready to talk books.

Nancy Kelly: Traveling Chef, Pellston, Michigan. (231) 539-7100.
Known throughout the culinary circles of northern Michigan for her private dinner party service and formal catering business. She's equally known in the same type of circles in Chicago. Trained in Paris, where she still spends part of every year, this would be a special treat to anyone's vacation.

Moving Mates, Stutsmanville Road at C-77, Stutsmanville. Many of the summer homes in this area are furnished with expensive items, many of them hard to duplicate. When owners who live in distant cities pass away these belongings usual are liquidated in estate sales. This company has found a niche in this resale market and insiders have been flocking to its sales barn since 1987 to pick up bargains and special treasures. It is only open on sales days though, so call in advance. 231-526-9265. Shopping here has a feel like Filene's Basement in Boston, so be ready.

Mankin's, U.S. 31 between Petoskey and Alanson.
This is the best sources for Great Lakes' fish and they supply many of the local restaurants in the area. An unassuming little building, but don't judge a book by its cover.

MUSEUMS AND SIGHTSEEING

Little Traverse History Museum. Petoskey.
There are good exhibits here on Hemingway, passenger pigeons, Petoskey stones and other aspects of life in this area.

The museum is housed in the former Chicago and West Michigan railroad depot, built in 1892. This is where tens of thousands of visitors to Petoskey entered the city from the late 19th Century until 1960, and the museum recaptures the time when this little station was one of the busiest in the North.

The museum reopened in the spring of 2004 after extensive renovation. It is located in Bayfront Park; accessible by way of W. Lake Street from U.S. 31 or by pedestrian tunnel from the downtown Gaslight District.

Open Monday to Saturday, June to September; Tuesday to Saturday, in May, October and November. Hours vary, so call in advance at (231) 347-2620. Admission charge.

Andrew Blackbird Museum. Harbor Springs.

His ancestry was Lakota, but Andrew J. Blackbird lived among the Ottawa and became their leading spokesperson and legal representative in the late 19th Century.

Educated at the Holy Childhood of Jesus Mission School in Harbor Springs, he led the Native American delegation to Washington, D.C., to negotiate the treaty of 1855.

His home, at 368 E. Main Street, Harbor Springs (which also was the town's first post office), is now a museum of Indian culture in the Little Traverse area with exhibits on crafts, customs and Ottawa history.

The museum is located just east of the business district, on Highway 119. It is open 10 a.m. to 4 p.m., Monday through Friday; during the summer months it also opens on Saturday, 10 a.m. to 2 p.m. Telephone is (231) 526-0612. A donation is asked.

Kilwin's Quality Confections. Petoskey.

If northern Michigan has one distinctive snack food item, it would probably be chocolate fudge. Stores selling the candy treat can be found in almost every resort in the area.

Among the most ubiquitous is Kilwin's, which started in Petoskey in 1947. It now has outlets throughout Michigan and eight other states and makes a wide assortment of candies and ice cream. If you are looking for fine chocolate, this is also the place to go—many hotels purchase these for special occasions.

Its main kitchen remains in Petoskey, at 355 N. Division Road, near the intersection with Mitchell St., east of downtown. Tours of the candy-making process, along with free samples, are offered during the summer at 10:30 and 11 in the morning and at 2 and 2:30 in the afternoon. Call in advance. (231) 347-3800.

Oden State Fish Hatchery. Oden.

Michigan has operated a trout hatchery in the Oden area since 1921. But in 2002, the old facility was shut down and a new one, among the most advanced in the

United States, opened nearby.

The $11 million project is the primary stocking facility for brown and rainbow trout in Michigan waters, both Great Lakes and inland. It is capable of planting more than one million fish a year. Visitors can tour the hatchery, the outdoor raceway which leads to open waters and the indoor broodstock building.

The old hatchery, meanwhile, has been turned into an interpretive center. There are exhibits on the Great Lakes watershed and how it works, an underwater viewing chamber that enables visitors to see what happens below the surface in a hatchery and a replica of a railroad car that was once used to transport fish. A short walking trail illustrates the workings of the watershed in the Crooked Lake area.

The old hatchery is located just off U.S. 31 in Oden at 8258 Ayr Road. It is open from 10 a.m. to 6 p.m., daily, Memorial Day to Labor Day.

To reach the new hatchery, drive south towards Conway on U.S. 31. Watch for North Conway Road on the right and turn there. At Powers Road, turn right again and make another right at Ayr Road. It is open Monday to Friday, 8:45 a.m. to 3:45 p.m. Admission is free to both facilities.

SEE-North Center for Outdoor Studies. Harbor Springs.
Opening in the fall of 2005, this is a place for an intimate look at the region's birds of prey. The Center was established by a local environmental group as a sanctuary for owls, hawks, eagles and falcons. Scientists observe their habits and visitors can observe the scientists observing the birds.

It's in a secluded location north of town. Take Highway 119 to Terpening Road, about 7 miles from Harbor Springs. Then left on Troup Road. (231) 348-9700. They also have a hands-on science exhibit in Petoskey that is worth a trip.

SEE-North Center for Outdoor Studies. Petoskey.
A natural history museum located downtown at 220 Park Avenue in Pennsylvania Park. It includes 21 interactive hands-on exhibits relating to northern Michigan. 10 a.m. to

4:30 p.m. Monday through Friday, 10:00 a.m. to 3:00 p.m. Saturday. Admission is $4.00 for adults.

Northern Michigan Hardwoods, Inc. Petoskey.

It's still possible to get a taste of the old lumbering days in the north. This company offers tours of its sawmill and hardwood plant and you can watch the logs being turned into flooring. There is also a gift shop offering crafted wood items.

The plant is off U.S. 31 on Townsend Road, opposite Bay Harbor, and then a right on Manthei Road. Tours are given by appointment only. (231) 347-4575.

Cross in the Woods. Indian River.

Since its dedication in 1954, this 55-foot high cross, carved from the trunk of a single Oregon redwood, has been one of the state's foremost religious attractions. The figure of Christ, sculpted by Michigan artist Marshall Fredericks, was added in 1959 and is 31 feet tall.

A shrine has grown up around the crucifix, believed to be the second largest in the world. There are gardens, grottoes and a museum of dolls in the costumes of various orders of nuns and priests. It is located in a suitably tranquil setting off M-68, just west of Burt Lake State Park. Services are held Monday to Friday, at 8:30 a.m. and noon; Saturday at 4:30 p.m. and Sunday at 8:30 a.m. and 10:30 a.m. Call (231) 238-8973.

BEACHES

A swim in this part of Lake Michigan, except for the occasional hot late summer afternoon, is bracing. Some would say ossifying. Nonetheless, there are some fine beach experiences in this area.

You can always find Petoskeys on the beach.

Petoskey State Park has the best stretch of sand, an absolutely beautiful facility with lots to do for swimmers, rockhounds and hikers.

At the far end of this site, unlikely as it now seems, used to be a foul-smelling leather tannery. The stream that flows into Little Traverse Bay here is still known as Tannery Creek, which actually isn't in the park. The land was acquired by Petoskey in 1934 and turned over to the state 34 years later. It now includes 304 acres with the dune-backed beach the main attraction. There is a changing house and concession stand in the park.

It is famous for its Petoskey stones, and a map, available at park offices, indicates where rock-hunting and metal-detecting are permissible. A trail leads to the top of Old Baldy dune for a panoramic view of the area. Another hiking path, Portage Trail, leads through the forested area of the park for a completely different outdoors experience.

The standard vehicle fee for state parks applies here.

Burt Lake State Park in Indian River has a sand beach that extends 2,000 feet along the lake's southern shore. Here's a helpful tip. Water in the inland lakes is always warmer than in Lake Michigan. Not by much, but enough to make a difference.

There are also concession stands and one mile of hiking trails in this facility, which has been a state park since 1920.

DeVoe Park, Indian River, is a little gem of a park situated at the mouth of the Indian River at Burt Lake. Take South Street west from the Straits Highway and follow the signs to the beach. There is a picnic area, changing rooms and a boardwalk that runs along the sand beach. It is also a popular gathering place for watching sunsets over the water.

Zoll Street Beach and Zorn Park in Harbor Springs run in vest-pocket parks that offer free, safe beaches for young children.

Zoll Street is on the eastern edge of town, and ends at the beach. There is a small parking area adjacent to it. Zorn Park is just west of downtown, running from Main Street, past Bay Street to Little Traverse Bay. Spectacular. It is somewhat larger, has a concession stand and a lifeguard during the season.

Thorne Swift Nature Preserve, north of Harbor Springs, is for those who want to avoid the crowds; this is the perfect beach experience. The 300-foot wide stretch of sand is located off Highway 119, five miles north of Harbor Springs. Watch for the turnoff to Lower Shore Drive and the Thorne Swift Preserve.

There is a nature center here, as well as a boardwalk trail and a dune observation deck. Brochures also guide visitors along the preserve's mile and a half of marked trails. Call ahead for workshops, this preserve is managed by the Little Traverse Conservancy. Naturalists are on duty but there are no lifeguards. A small parking fee is assessed for non-residents.

COUNTRY WALKS

The Thorne Swift facility is part of the Little Traverse Conservancy Nature Preserves, over 22,000 acres of land that has been protected for outdoor recreation. Three more of its parks are in this area.

Allan and Virginia McCune Preserve, east of Petoskey by way of Mitchell Road (C-58) and then south on Maxwell Road.

A one and a half mile trail loop follows Minnehaha Creek through a hardwood forest, rich in hemlock and cedar. It extends over 168 acres.

Round Lake Nature Preserve, just off Highway 119, two miles past the junction with U.S. 31, on Powell Road.

The park takes in 1,500 feet of the inland lake's shoreline. Wild roses can be found here and it is also the habitat of the pileated woodpecker.

Stutsmanville Bog Preserve, on State Road (C-77) just south of Stutsmanville Road, five miles north of Harbor Springs.

These wetlands are known for their unusual plants, including a few carnivorous species. The trail to the bog over-look is only one-quarter of a mile long but highly diverse in its animal and plant life.

Colonial Point Memorial Forest and Chaboiganig Nature Preserve, off Brutus Road, east of Brutus.

This 300-acre park preserves one of the oldest hardwood forests and the largest stand of first-growth red oak in the area. On a peninsula that extends into the western side of Burt Lake, the forest has been used by the University of Michigan as a research station since 1914. The land in the Preserve was almost sold for lumber twice, but the Conservancy managed to save it, for which anyone who walks through will be grateful. The Preserve has two and a half miles of hiking and ski trails in an irreplaceable ecological system.

Seven Springs Nature Preserve, west from the Straits Highway (Old U.S. 27) just north of Indian River on Prospect Road, then straight on Chippewa Beach Road.

There is a choice of two trails, both starting at the park-ing area. One heads up into a hardwood forest; the other descends a bluff through wetlands and emerges at the edge of Burt Lake. Each is about half a mile long. The springs which give the preserve its name are the habitat of the rare monkey flower, found in just 20 sites around the world.

Other Trails

Bear River Walkway, Petoskey.
It runs through the middle of town but you might as well be lost in the forest. The river drops 75 feet as it makes its way through Petoskey on the way to Little Traverse Bay, and the rush of falling water blocks out all other sounds.

You can enter it at Bayfront Park by taking the footpath below the U.S. 31 bridge. There is a short trail of about one mile that loops back on the far side of the river across a footbridge.

A more ambitious walk runs all the way to Sheridan Street at the southern edge of the city. There are benches along the route for rest stops and plenty of shade from the heavy growth of trees.

Petoskey Municipal Forest, Petoskey.
This property runs along the hills southeast of the city, embracing 800 acres of wooded area. Some of the views over the city and bay from the heights are magnificent. You get there by heading east from the middle of town on Greenwood Street. Turn right where it dead ends and follow this road, which becomes Brubaker. You will be able to access the forest either from here, Krause or King roads.

Wildwood Hills Pathway, Mackinaw State Forest.
A preferred choice of local hikers, the trails lead across 9.3 miles of thickly forested uplands on three loops of various lengths. Wildwood Road leads to the pathway parking area. Access from Petoskey is off C-58; from Indian River off the Straits Highway.

Lost Tamarack Pathway, Mackinaw State Forest.
The trailhead is at the Weber Lake Campground, with loops of one mile and three miles circling Weber and Little Weber lakes. A longer hike leads 1.25 miles to a parking

area along C-58, and then runs another 1.5 miles to link up with the Wildwood Trailway. Access from both Petoskey and I-75 is off C-58.

BIKING

A trail begins at the natural area of North Central Michigan College and runs across both flat and hilly terrain on back roads into the Mackinaw State Forest. The campus is at the end of Howard St., south from downtown. The trail, which is a link in the multi-state North Country Trail, can be accessed at the end of the college parking lot.

The most spectacular ride in this area, however, is the Little Traverse Wheelway, running all the way from Harbor Springs to Charlevoix. It is a destination spot for bikers. It is, for the most part, a non-taxing ride; 75 percent of it is flat with only 5 percent rated as steep. The occasional biker would have no problems over the vast majority of the route.

There is some gravel, but most of the wheelway is paved. Much of it runs along sidewalks or wide shoulders that parallel Highway 119 and U.S. 31. Some of the Petoskey segment goes through Bayfront Park and even into the Bay Harbor complex.

Both the Wildwood Hills and Little Tamarack pathways described in the previous section are highly esteemed as biking trails by the Top of Michigan Trails Council. This organization is also an excellent resource for maps and the latest trail information for biking as well as hiking and cross-country skiing. It is headquartered at 445 E. Mitchell St, Petoskey. Call (231) 348-8280.

Rentals

Four outlets offer bike rentals in the area:
Bahnhof Sports, on U.S. 31, just south of Bay View. (800) 253-7078.

High Gear Sports, at 1187 U.S. 31 North, Petoskey.
(231) 347-6118.

Latitude 45, at 476 W. Mitchell, Petoskey.
(231) 348-5342.
Touring Gear, at 108 E. Third St., Harbor Springs.
(231) 526-7152.

Most of these places also do repair work and offer trail
maps. Inquire in advance.

BOATING

Boating is very popular at Little Traverse Bay.

Cruising the Inland Waterway of Michigan is an unfor-
gettable small boat adventure, and the Alanson area is its
western outlet.

The route was used by Native Americans for centuries.
French trappers who followed them found it to be the safest
way to make the crossing from Lake Huron, avoiding the

treacherous Straits of Mackinac and leaving a portage of just two and a half miles to Lake Michigan. Then it was the course of the loggers. A small steamship, the *Topinabee,* carried day-trip passengers along the route in the early 20th Century.

Since 1957, after completion of a new 30-foot wide channel, it has become a way for pleasure boaters to enjoy a leisurely 38-mile trip across the top of Michigan's Lower Peninsula.

The Waterway begins at the Cheboygan River outlet into Lake Huron. It goes through Mullett Lake and the Indian River into Burt Lake. Finally it reaches this area by way of Crooked River and Crooked Lake. Because of the lock that connects Crooked River and Lake, navigation in this area is limited to boats of 25 feet and less.

There are two public access sites for boaters on Crooked Lake, which is also home to the North American Outboard Championships. One of them is just off U.S. 31, near Conway. The other is in the lake's southeastern corner. To reach it take Pickerel Lake Road east from U.S. 31, and then continue along the lake's southern shore on Channel Road.

Burt Lake is accessible from Burt Lake State Park, off M-68, just west of Indian River. There is another launch site at Maple Bay Campground, east of Brutus, on Brutus Road.

Boat Rentals

If you're not toting your own craft, there are several places between Oden and Alanson where pontoon boats, kayaks and canoes can be rented.

Spanky's is a good bet in Alanson. It's on River Street, at the swing bridge, one of the landmarks on the Crooked River. You can find pontoon and jet ski rentals there. (231) 548-4800.

In Oden, the **Windjammer Marina** and Sport Center, on Crooked Lake, is especially well supplied with all types of craft, even houseboats. It's located right on U.S. 31. (231) 347-6103.

About halfway between these two is the **Ryde Marina,** with an excellent assortment of kayaks and canoes. It's just south of Alanson, off U.S. 31. (248) 347-8273.

In the Burt Lake area, a good choice is the **Indian River Marina,** with a full rental line of pontoon, fishing and ski-towing boats. It is right on the river, north of town and east of the Straits Highway, at 3020 Apple Blossom Lane. (231) 238-9373.

Another possibility is the **Bear River Canoe Livery,** south of Petoskey. The Bear is a fine canoeing stream and the surroundings are a bit more rustic. From the middle of town, take Mitchell east to Kalamazoo, a right to Atkins, then a left to McDougal and straight on to the livery at 2517 McDougall. (231) 347-9038.

Rafting and Floating

The Sturgeon River is clocked as the fastest-flowing body of water in the Lower Peninsula, with a descent of 14 feet per mile, so a trip down the Sturgeon to its outlet at Burt Lake becomes one of the most exhilarating water adventures in this area.

Big Bear Adventures is the primary outfitter for canoe, kayak, tube and catamaran trips on the Sturgeon. Trips leave from its headquarters, at 4271 S. Straits Highway, opposite the boat launch at Burt Lake State Park, west of Indian River. It transports customers to one of several put-in points and they return to base on trips that range from 35-45 minutes (for rafts) to five hours (for canoes and kayaks).

The canoe and kayaking trips are not recommended for young children, but kids are encouraged on the shorter raft and tubing excursions. Prices start at $10 per person for the short tube trip. A minimum of four people is required for rafts.

Reservations should be made in advance at (231) 238-8181. Big Bear also offers, for the extremely hearty, winter raft trips.

FISHING

Long before anyone ever thought to swing a golf club or a tennis racket in this part of the world, fishing was the attraction that brought in the crowds. In Little Traverse Bay, Crooked Lake and the Bear and Maple rivers, its appeal continues unabated.

On the big lake, the prizes are trout, salmon and steelhead. Best bet for a day charter is the *Ruddy Duck II.* The boat is available for salmon and trout fishing and Capt. Barry Aspenleiter is an experienced guide. Call at (231) 347-3232.

There is also fishing off the Petoskey and Harbor Springs piers.

Crooked Lake, described in the previous section, is a good bet for walleye and smallmouth bass.

Local anglers really like the **Maple River.** This is a terrific trout stream in the area just south of Pellston. Check at the **Hidden River Golf and Casting Club** (800-325-4653) for tips on where the fish are. Fly fishing on the property is limited to just five people a day. It's just north of the town of Brutus and east of U.S. 31, at 7688 Maple River Road.

Or you might just want to park near the Brutus Road bridge across the Maple and try your luck there.

During the spring and autumn months, you can pull salmon out of the Bear River right in downtown Petoskey. Fishers gather at the Lake Street bridge.

Another good spot to hook up with a knowledgeable guide is **Whippoorwhill Fly Fishing.** Though they have closed their retail shops, they are still guiding. (231) 348-7061.

Burt Lake is an outstanding choice for walleye. Its southern area, between the outlets of the Sturgeon and Indian River, is known by fishing experts as "Walleye Alley." Smallmouth bass is another top game fish taken in these waters. Try the area off the mouth of the Maple River in the lake's western extremity, or Greenman Point on Boursau Bay, near its northeastern corner.

The **Sturgeon** is a fine trout stream and there is good access to it at the Haakwood Campground of Mackinaw State Forest, just off the Straits Highway, between Indian River and Wolverine.

GOLF

There are many great views from the golf courses.

In the last two decades, Emmet County has developed into one of the top golfing areas in the Midwest. The conventional wisdom had always been that this area was too far north, the season far too short, for the sport to gain a consistent following. That just goes to show how far you can trust conventional wisdom.

There are several major public operations here over a total of 13 courses and a few very private courses. Some of them are classics, rated exceptional by several golfing publications.

Bay Harbor Golf Club, Petoskey (231) 439-4028.

There are 27 holes over three courses here and golfers can combine any two to make a full round. The setting is spectacular. Course architect Arthur Hills calls it "The best piece of fresh water property ever devoted to golf design," and *Golfweek* describes it as "The most diverse collection of holes in America." Some of the holes run right beside the lakeshore, others are shaped around dunes and bluffs.

The **Links,** the Quarry (so named because several holes were constructed out of a former limestone pit) and the Preserve make up the choices. *Golf Magazine* rated this eighth out of the top 100 public courses in America.

It is also the costliest course in the area. Expect to pay around $200 for 18 holes; half of that for a twilight round after 5 p.m.

Boyne Highlands Resort, Harbor Springs.
(800) 462-6963.

There are four 18-hole courses on the property, with a range of difficulty that can accommodate every level of ability.

The **Heather Course** is the most challenging. This is a Robert Trent Jones design and it takes advantage of all the ridges and hollows of the hillside terrain. It is ranked as the best course on a Michigan resort by the authorities at *Golf Digest.*

The newest course is the **Hills,** named after its architect, Arthur Hills. Completed in 2000, it has quickly garnered a reputation for its hungry sand traps and water holes that can rattle even experienced golfers.

Each of these courses will cost around $129; twilight specials, kicking in at 4 p.m., are pegged at $59 on the Heather and $69 for the Hills.

The **Donald Ross Memorial** is an intriguing set-up, with 17 of the holes modeled after Ross designs around the world. The only exception is a hole recreated from Scotland's Royal Dornoch course, where Ross learned to play.

Ross was a pioneering architect of American courses in

the first half of the 20th Century. His best known achievement was Pinehurst, North Carolina, but many of the country's classic courses were inspired by his ideas.

Cost here is $109, with a $69 fee after 2 p.m.

The fourth course, the **Moor**, is noted for its water hazards. They come into play on 11 of its holes. The fee is $79, with a twilight cost of $49.

All the courses at Boyne Highlands and Bay Harbor, by the way, feature a water approach to the 18th hole. This was the unique signature of Everett Kircher, the resort owner who built the courses on both properties. He even over-rode the design of the masterful Jones on the Heather, his first course, to get the water where he wanted it.

Chestnut Valley Golf Club, Conway. (877) 284-3688. Left on North Conway Road from U.S. 31.

The course opened in 1994 and quickly became established as a favorite of golfers who relish a "north country" experience. That means its layout is set amid a hardwood forest and rolling terrain. *Golf Digest* gives it a 4-star rating.

Fee for 18 holes is $65-75, with a 9-hole option of $40-45; after 2 p.m. rates drop to $50-60 for 18 holes and $35-40 for 9.

Crooked Tree Golf Club, Petoskey. (800) 462-6963. On U.S. 31, opposite Bay Harbor.

The course is located on a ridge through pine and hardwood forest and the back nine open out on views of Little Traverse Bay. This is a less expensive option to the other courses on the Bay Harbor property and is operated by Boyne USA.

Fee is $79, and after 2 p.m. it drops to $49.

Harbor Point Golf Course, Harbor Springs. (231) 526-2951. North on Highway 119.

A genuinely historic course, opened in 1896, and for many years the exclusive preserve of the private Harbor Point Association. It remains semi-private, with the public permitted to tee off after 1:30 p.m. The setting is spectacular with many holes overlooking the bay. This is also noted as a fine walker's course, with carts not mandatory.

Fee is $66 for 18 holes and $33 for 9, including a cart. After 3 p.m. rates go down to $29 for 9 holes.

At the other end of Lake Road is Wequetonsing Golf Club, again over 100 years old, but very private. Only those with connections should try to play. A nice resort type course.

Hidden River Golf and Casting Club, Brutus.
(800) 325-GOLF. Off U.S. 31, at 7688 Maple River Road.

A river runs through it, which makes this a rather unique operation. It combines golf with fishing on one piece of property. Most challenging hole is the 636-yard 7th, with the green tucked in between two arms of a pond. Other holes run right alongside the water.

Fee is $85; after 3 p.m. it drops to $59.

Little Traverse Bay Golf Club, Harbor Springs.
(888) 995-6262. Off M-119 on West Conway Road, and an immediate left on Clayton Road. Straight ahead for two miles and then follow the signs up the hill.

Laid out among rolling hills in the middle of ski country. On some holes you tee off from the side of a bluff to reach the fairway. With views of the bay from one side of the course and Crooked Lake on the other, the scenery is as much a part of the experience as the golf. Opened in 1992, it's a four-star *Golf Digest* course and its restaurant is among the best in the area.

Fee is $80; after 3 p.m., $40.

Maple Ridge Golf Club, Brutus. (231) 529-6574.
North on U.S. 31. This is a family-friendly facility, with reasonable prices and two 18-hole courses. The redesigned championship course is somewhat more challenging, with several water holes coming into play. The executive course is smaller and flatter and a good choice to bolster the confi-

dence of beginners. A cart is not required.

Fee on both courses is $39 for 18 holes with cart; $20 for 9 holes, and $25 for 18 holes after 3 p.m.

Eagle Beach Golf Links, Alanson. (231) 548-9795. East from Alanson on M-68, then right on Banwell Road.

This is a work in progress as of this writing. The first nine of the proposed 18-hole course opened in 2002, and completion is still a few years away. The course was designed by Larry Mancour, a touring pro on the PGA circuit for 15 years and the architect of Chestnut Valley. The course occupies a great site, overlooking Pickerel Lake and includes five additional holes of par-3 golf.

The 18-hole fee is $32; 9 holes at $22; after 3 p.m., rates drop to $27 and $17.

True North Golf Club, Harbor Springs. (231) 526-3300. Five miles north of Harbor Springs at Stutsmanville and State roads.

This course opened in fall of 2004 and looks to fit in with the top courses in the area.

The 18-hole fee is $130, but call for seasonal rates.

The last course to talk about is **Bay View.** It is the first course you see when driving into Petoskey from the north, as it sits immediately next to U.S. 31. Nicely groomed as you would expect of a private club, it is not a taxing round, but the views are straight out to the water, and it would be part of a charming day at Bay View. Like Wequetonsing, you need connections to play here.

WINTER SPORTS

It was the success of downhill skiing in this part of Michigan that led to the creation of its golf resorts. Both were the work of Everett Kircher. A Studebaker dealer from Detroit, Kircher, who died in 2002, got tired of having to travel to New England or Colorado to pursue his favorite winter sport. He said later that he and a group of friends almost as a lark in 1947 bought the property that became Boyne Mountain, in neighboring Charlevoix County.

In doing so, he created the Midwestern ski industry, and this area remains its peak achievement. Boyne USA is now the largest family-owned resort company in the United States.

Boyne Highlands (800-GO-BOYNE), in the hills above Harbor Springs, was started by locals as Harbor Highlands and later purchased by Kircher's operation. It opened in 1964. It was here that he installed the first triple chair lift in the country and perfected the snow-making techniques that extended the season back to November and into April.

Boyne Highlands has the highest vertical drop (545 feet) in the area, the longest runs and the greatest skiable acreage. There are 54 slopes graded for all levels of ability. Experts go for the Couloir, the steepest in the Lower Peninsula. There are also 40 kilometers of groomed cross-country and snow-shoeing trails.

An ongoing Boyne tradition, instituted by Kircher, is to hire instructors from Austria, the birthplace of downhill skiing. Its snowsports school continues to do so and remains connected to the wellsprings of the sport.

Accommodations here are described in the Where to Stay section.

Nub's Nob (800-SKI-NUBS), which is known for its snowmaking, and in fact, its original 'snowmaker' Jim Dilworth, was the 'official snowmaker' for the Sarajevo Olympics in 1984. Nub's is perched on the hill immediately to the east, across Pleasantview Road, and is Boyne's main competitor in this area. It actually is six years older, opening in 1958, and has been named best overall ski resort in the Midwest by *Ski Magazine* for three consecutive years. (Boyne Highlands was sixth in the last tabulation.)

It is especially meticulous in its grooming, and remains the only Midwestern resort to finish in the top 10 of the magazine's poll on that aspect.

Chairlift overlooking Nub's Nob

Hamlet Village condominiums are located right next to its chairlifts. Reservations are handled by Land Masters at (800) 678-2341.

In addition to the large resorts, there is fine crosscountry skiing at many parks in the Petoskey area. Several trails begin at the natural area of **North Central Michigan College**, at the end of Howard Street, south of downtown.

Petoskey Municipal Forest also is a great area. Refer to the Country Hikes section for directions on how to get there.

Wildwood Hills and **Lost Tamarack** pathways in the **Mackinaw State Forest** also are prime cross-country areas. They are also described in the Country Hikes section.

River Road Sports Complex, a 60-acre park on the Bear River, offers more trails in the Bear River Valley. Take Sheridan St. east from U.S. 131. Turn right on Clarion, which becomes River Road.

For other snow activities, head for the city's **Winter Sports Park.** Petoskey is known for its championship high school ski teams and many of them began their training at this facility. There is a small ski slope, sledding hill and a rink for ice skating and hockey. Winter Park Lane runs off U.S. 31, just south of Bay View.

Harbor Springs has a dandy, low-key outdoor rink at 740 E. Main Street. It is open from 3-10 p.m. weekdays, noon to 10 p.m., Saturday, and noon to 8 p.m., Sunday.

OTHER ACTIVITIES

Pond Hill Farm, Harbor Springs.
A working farm that offers educational tours to demonstrate how things are done, agriculturally speaking. Activities are scheduled in the seasons other than dead of winter, including hay rides and scavenger hunts. A farm market displays products grown here.
Pond Hill is located at 5581 South Lake Shore, off M-119, north of town. Call 231-526-3276 for hours and a schedule of events.

Birchwood Farms Equestrian Center, Harbor Springs.
Everything related to getting around by horse; from lessons to carriage rides to winter sleigh rides. Hay rides and chuckwagon outings are also scheduled during the summer months.
The Center is located off Highway 119 on Stutsmanville Road, and then an immediate left on W. Townline Road. Call (231) 526-2868 for rates, reservations and scheduled events.
There is also an equestrian center at Bay Harbor, but it is private.

Wycamp Lake Club, Inc. Cross Village.
This hunting preserve is noted for its European-style pheasant hunts in autumn. Beaters drive the game birds into flight past hunters in blinds. The Club also organizes field hunts and operates an all-season shooting range.
It is northeast of Cross Village, by way of Lakeview and Wycamp roads. For reservations, rates and information call (231) 537-4830.

There are theater and concerts throughout the summer months at the **Bay View Association.** (231) 347-6225.

Free Concerts in the Park, ranging from big bands to chamber ensembles to country, are held in downtown Petoskey's Pennsylvania Park. They are scheduled at noon, on Tuesday and Friday, and at 7 p.m., Tuesday. (231) 347-4150.

Crooked Tree Arts Center puts on plays and has ongoing art shows. Located in downtown Petoskey, at 461 E. Mitchell. (231) 347-4337.

RAINY DAYS

The local movie house, **Petoskey Cinemas,** is a recently built multiplex, just off U.S. 131, one mile south of the junction with U.S. 31. Watch for the Anderson Road turnoff on the right. Call (231) 347-9696 for showtimes. Tuesday afternoons have special rates.

Petoskey Public Library is a stunning new facility, with a nice Hemingway collection, a huge children's reading room and an excellent collection on local history as well as less exalted reading material. This is a must visit. It's just off downtown at 500 E. Mitchell. (231) 347-4211.

Petoskey Public Library

Besides the outdoor center described in the Sightseeing section, **SEE-North** runs a small indoor exploration center, with inter-active displays on northern Michigan's natural habitat. There is also a gallery of local nature photography. It's located at 220 Park Avenue, a walkway that runs along-side downtown's Pennsylvania Park. (231) 348-9700.

If the kids contract cabin fever, try the **Jungle Indoor Family Fun Center,** with miniature golf and an arcade. Located next to the Big Boy restaurant, at the junction of U.S. 31 and 131.

There is also a new bowling alley on M-119 that will keep the rain off your head and the kids happy, and there are two places for indoor ice skating. The first is **Griffin Arena** (231-487-1843) at 3450 M-119 Harbor Springs and the second, **Polar Ice & Fitness,** which is an extensive work-out facility, including a room for only the ladies. Located at 611 Woodview in Petoskey (231-348-8480).

CASINO

Victories Casino is operated by the Little Traverse Bay Bands of Ottawa. It is a sports-themed place (appropriately enough, since it is housed in what was once a bowling alley). Of its 850 slots, more than 40 percent are of the nickel variety.

There are also the usual table games and craps. A deli, restaurant and show bar are on the premises, and the casino also runs a hotel with 137 rooms, an indoor pool and some excellent views of the bay.

Both the casino and hotel are located on U.S. 131, south of Petoskey. (231) 439-6100.

ANNUAL EVENTS

There are no blockbuster festivals that would be worth a special voyage to attend. But smaller events, many of them pitched to the seasons, give visitors plenty of diversions.

February:

Winter Carnival, Petoskey.
Held in the city's Winter Sports Park, with cardboard sled, ice skating and "bumpjumping" competitions. The last event is a form of downhill sled racing with a bump midway down that sends sleds flying. Dates vary from year to year. Call (231) 347-2500.

June:

Little Traverse Bay Historic Festival, Petoskey.
The third Saturday of the month is when local purveyors of good food get together to offer samples of their wares. Taste of the North is the most delectable part of this festival. There also is street entertainment, music, antique shows and special exhibits by the Little Traverse History Museum. 231-347-2620.

Sztuka, Cross Village.
A Polish arts festival, with traditional food, music and dancing. Sponsored by Legs Inn on the last Saturday of June to celebrate the ancestry of its founder. 231-526-2281.

Top o' Michigan Outboard Race, Indian River.
Its organizers call this marathon the 'world's toughest outboard race." The course runs across the Inland Waterway; through Crooked, Burt and Mullett lakes and their connecting rivers, with the pits situated at Indian River's DeVoe Park. The 2004 race was run in late June, but the date varies from year to year. Check with the Indian River Chamber of Commerce, at (800) 394-8310.

Lumberjack Festival, Wolverine.
This little town celebrates the tall timber days of the North with an annual jamboree. It features parades, home-made raft races, draft horse demonstrations, tug-o-wars and lumberjack games. It's usually held on the last weekend of the month. Call (231) 525-8653.

July:

Fourth of July, Harbor Springs.
There are many Independence Day observances in the area, but Harbor Springs puts on the best. There is a parade down Main Street, an art show and a dog-owner lookalike contest, among other frolics. (231) 526-7999.

Last weekend in July is the **Little Traverse Yacht Club Invitational Regatta,** known to all the locals as the "U-Gotta-Regatta." Photographers line up to capture this majestic site with 80-100 boats on the bay.

Antiques Festival, Petoskey.
Among the premier events of its kind in the North. Admission is charged. Usually scheduled on the first week-ends of July and August at the Emmet County Fairgrounds, west on U.S. 31. Call (231) 347-1010 for schedule.

Blissfest, Cross Village.
It's blues and it's bluegrass and it's a little touch of 60s rock festival, too. Blissfest has been going on for more than 20 years and has become a summertime standby. It is usually held over the second full weekend of July, but exact dates may vary. It's held on Division Road, off C-77. Call (231) 348-2815 for the latest information.

Art in the Park, Petoskey.
The most prestigious of the summer art shows, with a juried entry process and exhibits by some of the top artists and crafts workers in the state. Held the third Saturday of

July in downtown's Pennsylvania Park. Call the Petoskey Chamber of Commerce (231) 347-4150.

Summerfest, Indian River.
Started in 1981, this is a community-wide celebration of the season. There are events from the streets of downtown to the lakeshore at DeVoe Park, including sidewalk sales, craft shows and kids' games. It is usually held on the third weekend of the month.

Little Traverse Bay Regatta, Harbor Springs.
Even if you know little and care less about sailing, the sight of all those gleaming white sails on the blue waters of the bay will start your heart pumping. One of the great sights of summer. Last weekend in July. (231) 526-7919.

August:

Festival on the Bay, Petoskey.
This is a combination of a long goodbye to summer and a celebration of the sunsets that made Petoskey's reputation. (The name of the Ottawa chief for whom the city was named translates, by the way, as Sunrise. Go figure.) Music and art on the bayfront; on the third weekend of the month. Call the Petoskey Chamber of Commerce, (231) 347-4150.

Emmet County Fair, Petoskey.
A salute to the area's agrarian roots at the newly remodeled fairgrounds. Northern rural Michigan at its best. The last full week of August. Call (231) 347-1010 for schedule.

September:

Taste of Harbor Springs, Harbor Springs.
Harbor Spring's answer to the Petoskey tastefest held earlier in the summer. Local restaurants show what they can do. It goes on during the third Saturday of this month. Harbor Springs Chamber of Commerce, (231) 526-7999.

October:

Home Tour, Bay Harbor.
A chance to peek inside some of the huge homes in the Bay Harbor community. It is held in conjunction with a harvest festival. Second weekend of the month. Call the Little Traverse Historical Museum at (231) 347-2620 for details.

Up in Michigan, Petoskey.
The annual conference of Hemingway experts, who discuss the works of their favorite writer and examine his relationship with this area. Usually on the third weekend of the month, at Stafford's Perry Hotel. Call (231) 347-4000 for schedule of events.

HOSPITALS AND URGENT CARES

Northern Michigan Hospital, 416 Connable, Petoskey, (231) 487-4007. This hospital has an emergency room, but not an urgent care.

Petoskey Urgent Care, 1890 U.S. 131 South, Suite 4, (231) 487-2000. Across from Victories Casino, Monday through Friday, 8 a.m. to 6 p.m., Saturday and Sunday, 9 a.m. to 3 p.m.

Boyne Country Urgent Care, 1937 M-119 Highway, (231) 348-9200. Halfway between Harbor Springs and Petoskey and just south of Petoskey State Park, Monday through Friday, 9 a.m. to 9 p.m., Saturday and Sunday, 9 a.m. to 5 p.m.